Bundling

Its Origins, Progress, & Decline in America

by Henry Reed Stiles

Banned in Boston

1872

Chapman Billies, Inc.

Sandwich, Massachusetts

2004

ISBN 0-939218-23-2

This book is produced by
Chapman Billies, Inc.,
and distributed by
Alan C. Hood & Co., Inc.
P.O. Box 775
Chambersburg, PA 17201

PREFATORY.

IN the *History and Genealogies of Ancient Windsor, Conn.*, published in 1859, speaking of the influence of the old French wars upon the religious, moral and social life of New England, I used this language:

"Then came war, and young New England brought from the long Canadian campaigns, stores of loose camp vices and recklessness, which soon flooded the land with immorality and infidelity. The church was neglected, drunkenness fearfully increased, and social life was sadly corrupted. *Bundling*—that ridiculous and pernicious custom which prevailed among the young to a degree which we can scarcely credit—sapped the fountain of morality and tarnished the escutcheons of thousands of families."

Hereupon there came a buzzing around my

ears. Divers good sons of Connecticut winced under the soft impeachment of having a bundling ancestry, and intimated that my sketch of society in the olden times was somewhat overdrawn. In 1861, an esteemed antiquarian friend in Connecticut wrote me as follows: "Some of your friends feel that, in your *History of Windsor,* you showed too much inclination to malign, or at least ridicule, Connecticut institutions, though I think none of them accuse you of malice in the matter, and they fear that this subject of bundling cannot be ventilated without endangering the fair fame of old Connecticut."

Upon that hint I speak. Although born in the city of New York, I am the son of Connecticut parents, and proud to trace my descent through six generations of honest, hard-working God-fearing Connecticut yeomanry. By the mere accident of birth I cannot feel myself absolved from that allegiance to the Wooden Nutmeg State, which is imposed upon me by the ties of ancestry, of relationship, of youthful associations, and last, not least, by the deep interest which I have taken in the history of one of its eldest-born towns. I am, indeed, at this day, to all intents and purposes, as wholly and truly a Connecticut man as if born within her borders; and as proud of her past, as hopeful of her future, and as jealous of her reputation as any one could desire. I trust, therefore, that I may be allowed to disclaim any "inclination to malign, or at least ridicule Connecticut institutions," a task which, in my case, would savor of ingratitude, and which I should consider unworthy of my humble pen.

I cannot but think, also, that those who have found, or think that they have found, an inimical design in any pleasantries in which I may have indulged while describing the customs and manners of by-gone days—have betrayed a *thin-skinnedness,* and an ignorance of the true glory of Connecticut history, when they imagine that her fair fame can be seriously tarnished by the fly-specks of certain customs—at no time without their vigorous opponents—and long since rendered obsolete by the march of improvement.

The fun of the thing, however, is, that the sentence which has thus called forth the animadversions of the critics, will be found, with its context, on closer examination, to have applied to the *New England Colonies,* and not to Connecticut alone! In their haste to vindicate the land of steady habits, they seem to have assumed more than their share of the reproach involved in my simple historical statement.

As for myself, I am no believer in the theory that the objectionable portions of history should be kept in the background, and that only the bright side should be turned towards the world. If, as one has happily said, "history is experience teaching by example," we most surely need to have both sides fairly presented to us, before we can properly extract therefrom the lesson of good or of evil which is therein taught. It is unnecessary to pursue the argument further.

Suffice it to say, that perfection is as little to be expected in the history of a state or a community, as in the life of an individual. As to our ancestors, we must take them as history shows them to us—"men of like passions with ourselves," and "in all respects tempted as we are," yet neither worse, nor, again, very much purer or better than ourselves.

In this spirit I have undertaken to trace, in the following pages, the origin, progress and decline of the custom of bundling in America, together with such facts as clearly prove that it was not confined to this continent, but prevalent in various countries of the world.

"Honi Soit qui mal y pense."

H. R. S.

Albany, 1871.

BUNDLING.

BUNDLING. "A man and a woman lying on the same bed with their clothes on; an expedient practiced in America on a scarcity of beds, where, on such occasions, husbands and parents frequently permitted travelers to *bundle* with their wives and daughters."—*Grose, Dictionary of the Vulgar Tongue.*

BUNDLE, *v. i.* "To sleep on the same bed without undressing; applied to the custom of a man and woman, especially lovers, thus sleeping."—*Webster,* 1864.

BUNDLE, *v. n.* "To sleep together with the clothes on."—*Worcester,* 1864.

BUNDLING, as may be seen from the above quoted definitions, was practiced in two forms: first, between *strangers,* as a simple domestic make-shift arrangement, often arising from the necessities of a new country, and by no means peculiar to America; and, secondly, between *lovers,* who shared the same couch, with the mutual understanding that innocent endearments should not be exceeded. It was, however, in either case, a custom of convenience.

We may notice, in this connection, that it is very common, even at the present day, in New England, to speak of one as having "bundled in with his clothes on," if he goes to bed without undressing; as, for instance, if he came home drunk, or feeling slightly ill, lay down in the daytime, or in a cold night found the blankets too scanty.

The point which first claims our attention in the discussion of this custom, is its probable *origin,* and its *antiquity* in

THE BRITISH ISLES.

For, though British travelers have uniformly endeavored to fix the odium of this custom upon us, their transatlantic cousins, as being peculiarly "an American institution," it is, nevertheless, an indisputable fact that bundling has for centuries flourished within their own kingdom. For what else, in fact, was that universal custom of promiscuous sleeping together which prevailed among the ancient Britons at the time of the Roman conquest, and which led Cæsar to consider them as polyandrous polygamists, and other ancient writers to give them an unenviable character for morality? * Bundling, of course! in its rudest aboriginal form.

As to its moral aspects, being more charitably inclined towards our British friends than they oftentimes are to us, we are willing to accept Logan's defense of their ancestors. "The custom," he says, "which continued until lately in

---

* *Cæsar* says, that several brothers, or a father and his sons, would have but one wife among them. *Solinus,* indeed, says that the women in Thule were common, the king having a free choice; and *Dio* says the Caledonians had wives in common; yet these assertions may well be disputed. *Strabo* describes the Irish as extremely gross in this matter; *O'Connor* says polygamy was permitted; and *Derrick* tells us they exchanged wives once or twice a year; while *Campion* says they only married for a year and a day, sending their wives home again for any slight offense.—*Logan's Scottish Gael,* 5th Am. ed., p. 472.

some parts, and yet exists among a few of the rudest, who sleep altogether on straw or rushes, according to the general ancient practice, there is reason to believe, led to the aspersion cast on the British and Irish tribes. How natural it must have been for a casual observer to suppose, from seeing men and women reposing in the same place, that the marriage rites were not in force. To judge of the ancient inhabitants by the rudest of the present Highlanders and Irish, who often sleep in the same apartment, and are sometimes exposed to each other in a state of semi-nudity, we should not come to a conclusion unfavorable to their morality,*

* *A History of the Highlands, and of the Highland Clans*, etc., (Jas. Browne, LL.D., Advocate, 4 vols. London, 1853), IV, 398.

"The law of marriage observed in the Highlands has frequently been as little understood as that of succession, and similar misconceptions have prevailed regarding it. This was, perhaps, to be expected. In a country where a bastard son was often found in undisturbed possession of the chiefship or property of a clan, and where such bastard generally received the support of the clansmen against the claims of

for this mode of life is not productive of that
conjugal infidelity which St. Jerome and others

---

the feudal heir, it was natural to suppose that very loose
notions of succession were entertained by the people; that
legitimacy conferred no exclusive rights; and that the title
founded on birth alone might be set aside in favor of one
having no other claim than that of election. But this, al·
though a plausible, would nevertheless be an erroneous supposition. The person here considered as a bastard, and described as such, was by no means viewed in the same light by
the Highlanders, because, according to their law of marriage,
which was originally very different from the feudal system
in this matter, his claim to legitimacy was as undoubted as
that of the feudal heir afterwards became. It is well known
that the notions of the Highlanders were peculiarly strict in
regard to matters of hereditary succession, and that no people on earth was less likely to sanction any flagrant deviation
from what they believed to be the right and true line of
descent. All their peculiar habits, feelings and prejudices
were in direct opposition to a practice which, had it been
really acted upon, must have introduced endless disorder and
confusion, and hence the natural explanation of this apparent anomaly seems to be, what Mr. Skene has stated, namely,
that a person who was feudally a bastard might in their view
be considered as legitimate, and therefore entitled to be supported in accordance with their strict ideas of hereditary
right, and their habitual tenacity of whatever belonged to
their ancient usages. Nor is this mere conjecture or hy-
pothesis. A singular custom regarding marriage, retained

insinuate as prevalent among the old Scots.
* * * Nations that are even in a savage state

---

till a late period amongst the Highlanders, and clearly indi-
cating that their law of marriage originally differed in some
essential points from that established under the feudal system, seems to afford a simple and natural explanation of the
difficulty by which genealogists have been so much puzzled.

"This custom was termed *hand-fasting,* and consisted in
a species of contract between two chiefs, by which it was
agreed that the heir of one should live with the daughter of
the other as her husband for twelve months and a day. If,
in that time, the lady became a mother, or proved to be
with child the marriage became good in law, even although
no priest had performed the marriage ceremony in due form;
but should there not have occurred any appearance of issue,
the contract was considered at an end, and each party was at
liberty to marry or hand-fast with any other. It is manifest
that the practice of so peculiar a species of marriage must
have been in terms of original law among the Highlanders,
otherwise it would be difficult to conceive how such a custom
could have originated, and it is in fact one which seems naturally to have arisen from the form of their society, which
rendered it a matter of such vital importance to secure the
lineal succession of their chiefs. It is perhaps not improbable
that it was this peculiar custom which gave rise to the report
handed down by the Roman and other historians, that the
ancient inhabitants of Great Britain had their wives in common, or that it was the foundation of that law of Scotland
by which natural children became legitimatized by subse-

are sometimes found more sensitive on that
point of honor than nations more advanced in

---

quent marriage. And as this custom remained in the Highlands until a very late period, the sanction of ancient custom
was sufficient to induce them to persist in regarding the offspring of such marriages as legitimate."

It appears, indeed, that as late as the sixteenth century,
the issue of a hand-fast marriage claimed the earldom of
Sutherland. The claimant, according to Sir Robert Gordon,
described himself as one lawfully descended from his father,
John, the third earl, because, as he alleged, "his mother was
hand-fasted and fianced to his father;" and his claim was
bought off (which shows that it was not considered as altogether incapable of being maintained) by Sir Adam Gordon,
who had married the heiress of Earl John. Such, then, was
the nature of the peculiar and temporary connection which
gave rise to the apparent anomalies which we have been considering. It was a custom which had for its object, not to
interrupt but to preserve the lineal succession of the chiefs,
and to obviate the very evil of which it is conceived to afford
a glaring example. But after the introduction of their
feudal law, which, in this respect, was directly opposed to
the ancient Highland law, the lineal and legitimate heir, according to Highland principles, came to be regarded as a
bastard by the government, which accordingly considered
him as thereby incapacitated for succeeding to the honors and
property of his race; and hence originated many of those dis-
putes concerning succession and chiefship, which embroiled
families with one another, as well as with the government,

civilization; and all, perhaps, that can be admitted is, that certain formalities may have been practiced by the Britons, from which the *bundling* of the Welsh, and the *hand-fasting* in some parts of Scotland, are derived. The conversation which took place between the Em-

---

and were productive of incredible disorder, mischief and bloodshed. No allowance was made for the ancient usages of the people, which were probably but ill understood; and the rights of rival claimants were decided according to the principles of a foreign system of law, which was long resisted, and never admitted except from necessity. It is to be observed, however, that the Highlanders themselves drew a broad distinction between bastard sons and the issue of the hand-fast unions above described. The former were rigorously excluded from every sort of succession, but the latter were considered as legitimate as the offspring of the most regularly solemnized marriage.

This practice obtained not only among chiefs, but common people.

Walter Scott, in the xxv chapter of the *Monastery,* in a note, says: "This custom of hand-fasting actually prevailed in the upland days. It arose partly from the want of priests. While the convents subsisted, monks were detached on regular circuits through the wilder districts, to marry those who had lived in this species of connexion. A practice of the same kind existed in the Isle of Portland."

press Julia and the wife of a Caledonian chief, as related by Xiphilin, certainly evinces a grossness and indelicacy in the amours of the British ladies, if true; but it appears to be a reply where wit and reproof were more aimed at than truth. The case of the Empress Cartismandua shows the nice feeling of the Britons as to the propriety of female conduct. The respect of the Germans for their females, and the severity with which they visited a deviation from virtue, have been described; and the further testimony of Tacitus may be adduced, who says that but very few of the greatest dignity chose to have more than one wife, and when they did it was merely for the honor of alliance. It may be here stated that the Gaëls have no word to express cuckold, and that prostitutes were, by Scots' law, like that of the ancient Germans, thrown into deep wells; and a woman was not permitted to complain of an assault if she allowed more than one night to elapse before the accusation."—*Logan's*

Scottish Gael, 5th American edition, p. 472.*

Indeed, whatever may have been the real state of morality among the ancient Scotch and Irish—and it is quite probable that it has been unfairly depicted by casual and prejudiced observers—the ancient custom of bundling, which has been handed down from earliest times, has not greatly contaminated their descendants of the present day. For, whatever their national vices, the Scotch and Irish of our day maintain a character for chastity superior to that of many

---

* In *Scottish Ballads and Songs,* by James Maidment, Edinburg, MDCCCLIX, under the title of *Luckidad's Garland,* p. 134, is a remarkable picture of the old and new times in Scotland, eighty or ninety years ago, three of the twenty-four verses of which the ballad is composed, being descriptive of something akin to *bundling.* In a London edition of *Hudibras,* also, published in 1811, is a note to line 913, of Part I, Canto I. As both of these extracts, however, are somewhat too *broad* for our pages, we content ourselves with simply referring thereto. In the same category, also, is the definition, in *Bailey's Old English Dictionary,* of the term *free bench,* as prevailing in the manors of East and West Embourn, Chaddleworth in the county of Berks, Tor in Devonshire, and other places of the west.

of their more fortunate and more civilized neighbors. Bundling, as now practiced in these kingdoms, is merely a matter arising from the ignorance, or the poverty of the inhabitants; and, while not salutary in its moral or physical influence, is, at all events, less abused than we might reasonably expect.

In regard to

WALES.

We learn from Woodward's admirable history of that kingdom, the following facts concerning the domestic habits of its people in the twelfth century:

"At night a bed of rushes was laid down along one side of the room, covered with a coarse kind of cloth, made in the country, called *brychan;* and all the household lay down on this bed in common, without changing their dresses. The fire was kept burning through the night, and the sleepers maintained their warmth by lying closely; and when, by the hardness of their couch, one side was wearied, they would get up and sit by the fire awhile, and then lie down again on the other side. It is to this custom of promiscuous sleeping, that some of the worst habits of the Welsh at the present day may be ascribed; and from the same custom which their forefathers, the ancient Britons, practiced, arose Cæsar's supposition that they were polyandrous polygamists."

These habits, which were a matter of necessity with the ancient Welsh, have become converted, by the lapse of time, among their descendants of the present day, into an amatory custom precisely similar to that practiced formerly in New England.*

---

* *History of Wales* (by B. B. Woodward, B.A., London, 1853), p. 320; who adds, also, p. 186, the following:

"The laws which treat of the violation of the marriage bond and those which relate to chastity generally, recognize a degree of laxity respecting female honor, and, yet more remarkably, an absence of feminine delicacy, such as could scarcely be paralleled amongst the most uncivilized

A tourist through Wales, in the year 1797,[*] thus speaks of the Welsh *bundling*: "And here, amongst the usages and customs, I must not omit to inform you that what you have, perhaps, often heard, without believing, respecting the *mode of courtship* amongst the Welsh peasants, is true. The lower order of people do actually carry on their love affairs in bed, and what would extremely astonish more polished lovers, they are carried on honorably, it being, at least, as usual for the Pastoras of the mountains to go from the bed of courtship to the bed of marriage as unpolluted and maidenly as the

---

people now. They are of such a nature, that though most characteristic, they must be passed by with this general mention. The distinction between the Celtic and Teutonic races is perhaps in no case more plainly marked than in this: The Anglo-Saxon laws on this subject (always excepting those of the *ecclesiastical* authorities) are modesty itself, notwithstanding their plain speaking, compared with those of the Welsh legislators."

[*] *Gleanings through Wales, Holland, and Westphalia,* etc. (3rd edition, by Mr. Pratt, London, 1797), I, pp. 105-107.

Chloes of fashion; and yet you are not to conclude that this proceeds from their being less
susceptible of the *belle-passion* than their
betters; or that the cold air which they breathe
has frozen 'the genial current of their souls.'
By no means; if they cannot boast the voluptu-
ous languor of an Italian sky, they glow with
the bracing spirit of a more invigorating at-
mosphere. I really took some pains to investigate this curious custom, and after being
assured, by many, of its veracity, had an opportunity of attesting its existence with my own
eyes. The servant maid of the family I visited
in Caernarvonshire, happened to be the object
of a young peasant, who walked eleven long
miles every Sunday morning to favor his suit,
and regularly returned the same night through
all weathers, to be ready for Monday's employ-
ment in the fields, being simply a day laborer.
He usually arrived in time for morning service,
which he constantly attended, after which he
escorted his Dulcinea home to the house of her

master, by whose permission they as constantly passed the succeeding hour in bed, according to the custom of the country. These tender sabbatical preliminaries continued without interruption near two years, when the treaty of alliance was solemnized; and, so far from any breach of articles happening in the meantime, it is most likely that it was considered by both parties as a matter of course, without exciting any other idea. On speaking to my friend on the subject, he observed that, though it certainly appeared a dangerous mode of making love, he had seen so few *living* abuses of it, during six and thirty years' residence in that country, where it nevertheless had always, more or less, prevailed, he must conclude it was as innocent as any other. One proof of its being *thought* so by the parties, is the perfect ease and freedom with which it is done; no awkwardness or confusion appearing on either side; the most well-behaved and decent young woman going into it without a blush, and they are by no means deficient in modesty. What is pure in idea is always so in conduct, since bad actions are the common consequence of bad thoughts; and though the better sort of people treat this ceremony as a barbarism, it is very much to be doubted whether more *faux pas* have been committed by the Cambrian boors in this *free access* to the bed chambers of their mistresses than by more fashionable Strephons and their nymphs in groves and shady bowers. The power of habit is perhaps stronger than the power of passion, or even of the charms which inspire it; and it is sufficient, almost, to say a thing is the *custom of a country,* to clear it from any reproach that would attach to an innovation. Were it the practice of a few only, and to be gratified by stealth, there would, from the strange construction of human nature, be more cause of suspicion; but being ancient, general, and carried on without difficulty, it is probably as little dangerous as a *tête à tête* in a drawing-room, or in any other full dress place where young people meet to say soft things to each other."

In an antiquarian tour by the Rev. W. Bingley, in 1804,* we also find the following description of this custom: "The peasantry of part of Caernarvonshire, Anglesea, and Merionethshire, adopt a mode of *courtship* which, till within the last few years, was scarcely even heard of in England. It is the same that is common in many parts of America, and termed by the inhabitants of that country, *bundling*. The lover steals, under the shadow of the night, to the bed of the fair one, into which (retaining an essential part of his dress) he is admitted without any shyness or reserve. Saturday or Sunday nights are the principal times when this courtship takes place, and on these nights the men sometimes walk from a distance of ten miles or more to visit their favorite damsels.

---

* *North Wales, including its Scenery, Antiquities, Customs*, etc. (by Rev. W. W. Bingley, A.M., 2 vols., 8vo, London, 1804), II, p. 282.

This strange custom seems to have originated in the scarcity of fuel, and in the unpleasantness of sitting together in the colder part of the year without a fire. Much has been said of the innocence with which these meetings are conducted, but it is a very common thing for the consequence of the interview to make its appearance in the world within two or three months after the marriage ceremony has taken place. The subject excites no particular attention among the neighbors, provided the marriage be made good before the living witness is brought to light. Since this custom is entirely confined to the laboring classes of the community, it is not so pregnant with danger as, on a first supposition, it might seem. Both parties are so poor that they are necessarily constrained to render their issue legitimate, in order to secure their reputation, and with it a mode of obtaining a livelihood."

Another traveler * also mentions "a singular custom that is said to prevail in Wales, relating

to their mode of courtship, which is declared
to be carried on in bed; and, what is more
extraordinary, it is averred that the moving
tale of love is agitated in that situation without
endangering a breach in the preliminaries."
Referring to Mr. Pratt's account of the custom,
before quoted, he proceeds to remark: "Our
companion, like every one else that we spoke
with in Wales on the subject, at once denied
the existence of this custom: that maids in many
instances admitted male bed-fellows, he did not
doubt; but that the procedure was sanctioned
by *tolerated* custom he considered a gross misrepresentation. Yet in Anglesea and some parts
of North Wales, where the original simplicity
of manners and high sense of chastity of the
natives is retained, he admitted *something of the
kind* might appear. In those thinly inhabited
districts a peasant often has several miles to

---

* *A Tour throughout North Wales and Monmouthshire,*
etc., etc. (by J. T. Barbor, F.S.A., London, 1803), pp.
103-9.

walk after the hours of labor, to visit his mistress; those who have reciprocally entertained the *belle passion* will easily imagine that before the lovers grow tired of each other's company the night will be far enough advanced; nor is it surprising that a tender-hearted damsel should be disinclined to turn her lover out over bogs and mountains until the dawn of day. The fact is, that under such circumstances she admits a *consors lecti,* but not in *nudatum corpus.* In a lonely Welsh hut this bedding has not the alarm of ceremony; from sitting, or perhaps lying, on the hearth, they have only to shift their quarters to a heap of straw or fern covered with two or three blankets in a neighboring corner. The practice only takes place with *this view of accommodation.*"

Still another glimpse of this favorite Welsh custom is presented by a tourist in 1807.* He says:

---

* *The Stranger in Ireland,* by John Carr.

"One evening, at an inn where we halted, we heard a considerable bustle in the kitchen, and, upon enquiry, I was let into a secret worth knowing. The landlord had been scolding one of his maids, a very pretty, plump little girl, for not having done her work; and the reason which she alleged for her idleness was, that her master having locked the street door at night, had prevented her lover enjoying the rights and delights of *bundling,* an amatory indulgence which, considering that it is sanctioned by custom, may be regarded as somewhat singular, although it is not exclusively of Welsh growth. The process is very simple; the gay Lothario, when all is silent, steals to the chamber of his mistress, who receives him in bed, but with the modest precaution of wearing her under petticoat, which is always fastened at the bottom—not unfrequently, I am told, by a sliding knot. It may astonish a London gallant to be told that this extraordinary experiment often ends in a downright wedlock—

the knot which cannot slide. A gentleman of respectability also assured me that he was obliged to indulge his female servants in these nocturnal interviews, and that too at all hours of the night, otherwise his whole family would be thrown into disorder by their neglect; the carpet would not be dusted, nor would the kettle boil. I think this custom should share the fate of the northern Welsh goats. * * * Habit has so reconciled the mind to the comforts of *bundling,* that a young lady who entered the coach soon after we left Shrewsbury, about eighteen years of age, with a serene and modest countenance, displayed considerable historical knowledge of the custom, without one touch of bashfulness."*

* "On his way to Ireland he passed through Wales, and gives us a slight sketch of the character of that people and country. *It must afford no small gratification to a New England man to learn that the practice of* BUNDLING *is not peculiar to us, but that this pleasing though dangerous art was probably imported from abroad.*"—A review of *The Stranger in Ireland,* in *Connecticut Courant* for November 19th, 1806.

Thus much for Wales, where the custom seems to have been entirely confined to the lower classes of society, and where we have reason to think it still prevails to some extent to this day.†

The same author whom we last quoted also speaks of a "courtship similar to *bundling*, carried on in the islands of Vlie and Wieringen,

---

† In this connection we may give the following extract from *Ancient Laws and Institutes of Wales,* etc., etc., printed by command of his late Majesty King William IV, under the direction of the commissioners on the Public Records of the Kingdom. MDCCCXLI. Folio. From page 369.—The Gwentian Code.

"A woman of full age who goes with a man clandestinely, and taken by him to bush, or brake, or house, and after connection deserted; upon complaint made by her to her kindred, and to the courts, is to receive, for her chastity, a bull of three winters, having its tail well shaven and greased and then thrust through the door-clate; and then let the woman go into the house, the bull being outside, and let her plant her foot on the threshold, and let her take his tail in her hand, and let a man come on each side of the bull; and if she can hold the bull, let her take it for her *wynet-werth* [face-shame] and her chastity; and, if not, let her take what grease may adhere to her hands."

In Holland

Under the name of *queesting*.* At night the lover has access to his mistress after she is in bed; and, upon an application to be admitted upon the bed, which is of course granted, he raises the quilt, or rug, and in this state *queests,* or enjoys a harmless chit-chat with her, and then retires. This custom meets with the perfect sanction of the most circumspect parents, and the freedom is seldom abused. The author traces its origin to the parsimony of the people, whose economy considers fire and candles as superfluous luxuries in the long winter evenings."

---

* A good honest word, which although not exactly English, is at least first cousin to our *quest,* and *quiz,* etc.

Worcester gives the following: "Quese, *v. a.,* to search after. *Milton."* Quest, *v. n.,* to join search. *B. Jonson.* Quester, *n.,* a seeker. *Rowe.*

Is it not allowable to derive from one of these words Quesing, or Questing, pronounced Qweesting, and from the other Questing? So that he who went *queesting* was simply *searching after* a wife, understood.

The Hon. Henry C. Murphy of Brooklyn, N. Y., late United States minister at the Hague, has furnished us with the following note in relation to this Nederduitsche custom: "As to its being a Dutch custom, it was so to a limited extent in Holland in former times, and may yet be, though I did not hear of it when I was there. Sewell gives the word *queesten,* or *kweesten,* in his dictionary, printed over a century ago. The word is defined in the dictionary of Wieland, the principal lexicographer in that country, as follows: '*Kweesten*. Upon the islands of Texel and Vlieland* they use this word for a singular custom of wooing, by which the doors and windows are left open, and the lover, lying or sitting outside the covering, woos the girl who is underneath.' Sewell confines the custom to certain islands or lands near the sea."

---

* These are two very small islands at the opening of the Zuider zee.

LOVE AND COURTSHIP IN THE 14TH CENTURY

In feudal times, in the last part of the four-
teenth century, it became the practice for the
vassals, or feudatories, to send their sons to be
educated in the family of the suzerain, while
the daughters were similarly placed with the
lady of the castle. These formed a very im-
portant part of the household, and were of
gentle blood, claiming the honorary title of
chambrières or chamber-maidens. The dem-
oiselles of this period were very susceptible to
the passion of love, which was the ruling spirit
of the inmates of the castle. Feudal society
was, in comparison to the previous times,
polished and even brilliant, but it was not,
under the surface, pure. Many good maxims
were taught, but they were not all practiced.
"There was an extreme intimacy between the
two sexes, who commonly visited each other in
their chambers or bedrooms. Thus in the poem
of Guatier d'Aupias, the hero is represented as

visiting in her chamber the demoiselle of whom he is enamored. Numerous similar examples might be quoted. At times, one of the parties is described as being actually in bed, as is the case in the romance of *Blonde of Oxford,* where Blonde visits Jehan in his chamber when he is in bed, and stays all night with him, in perfect innocence as we are told in the romance. We must remember that it was the custom in those times for both sexes to go to bed perfectly naked."*

IN SWITZERLAND,

According to an English observer,† analogous modes of courtship still exist. In speaking of the canton *Unterwald* he says: "In the story of

---

* From *The Student and Intellectual Observer,* London, November number, 1868, p. 310, in an article by Thomas Wright, F.S.A. Chapter vii—*Womankind in all Ages of Western Europe,* etc.

† *Cottages of the Alps* (London, 1860), pages 77, 91, 132.

the destruction of the castles, we read that the surprise was effected by a young girl admitting her lover to her room by a ladder, and an English guide-book remarks, that this is still the fashion of receiving lovers in Switzerland. Reference is had to the manner of wooing, which in some cantons is called *lichtgetren,* in others *dorfen* and *stubetegetren,* and answers to the old-fashioned *going-a-courting* in England. The customs connected with it vary in different cantons, but exist in some form in all except two or three.

"In the canton *Lucerne,* the *kiltgang* is the universal mode of wooing; the lover visiting his betrothed in the evening, to be pelted on the way by all mischievous urchins; or if he is seated quietly with her by the winter fire, they are sure to be serenaded by all manner of *cat voices* under the window, which are continued till he issues forth, perhaps at dawn in the morning; and however long may be a courtship, these *cater-waulings* are the invariable

attendants, and not the most lamentable consequences of these nightly visits, recognized, however, as entirely respectable and conventional in
every canton."

And again in the canton *Vaud,* he says, "the
kiltgang, or nightly wooings, are the universal
custom with the universal consequences, but in
general the wife is treated with marked respect,
is made keeper of the treasury, and consulted
as the oracle of the family."

Among the amatory customs of various

SAVAGE NATIONS

and tribes, there are certain which somewhat
resemble *bundling,* except in the greater degree
of freedom allowed—a freedom which, in the
eyes of civilized nations, is absolute immorality.
Of this description is the manner of wooing described by La Hontan as prevalent among the
Indians of North America.*

---

* *New Voyage to North America, giving a full Account*

Yet, in many of these instances, if we were to carefully examine the social system and customs of our savage friends, and were willing to judge them rather by the results of our own observation, than by our preconceived opinions, we should probably find that the absolute *practical morality* of these *untutored natives,* was quite equal, if not superior, to that of the educated and civilized whites.*

---

of the Customs, Commerce, Religion and Strange Opinions of the Savages of that Country, etc., etc. Written by the Baron Lahontan, Lord Lieutenant of the French Colony at *Placentia,* in Newfoundland, now in England. London, 1703.

In describing the amatory customs of the Indians of this country, the author says (Vol. II, p. 37):

"You must know further, that Two Hours after Sun-set the Old Superannuated Persons, or Slaves (who never lie in their Masters' Huts) take care to cover up the Fire before they go. 'Tis then that the Young Savage comes well wrapt up to his Mistress's Hut, and lights a sort of a Match at the Fire; after which he opens the Door of his Mistress's Apartment and makes up to her bed: If she blows out the light he lies down by her; but if she pulls her Covering over her Face, he retires; that being a Sign that she will not receive him."

Among these *customs de amour,* however, to which we have alluded as existing among different savage tribes, there are none which bear so perfect a resemblance to *bundling,* as that described by Masson in his *Journeys in Central Asia, Belochistan, Afghanistan,* etc. (III, 278.) He says:

"Many of the Afghan tribes have a custom of wooing similar to what in Wales is known as *bundling-up,* and which they term *namzat bezé.* The lover presents himself at the house of his betrothed with a suitable gift, and in return is allowed to pass the night with her, on the under-

---

* Verily, Peters's sarcasm savors as much of truth as humor when, speaking of bundling, he says: "The Indians who had this method of courtship among them in 1634, are the most chaste set of people in the world. Concubinage and fornication are vices none of them are addicted to, except such as forsake the laws of Hobbamockon and turn Christians. The savages have taken many female prisoners, carried them back three hundred miles into their country, and kept them several years, and yet not a single instance of their violating the laws of chastity has ever been known. This cannot be said of the French, or of the English, whenever Indian or other women have fallen into their hands."

standing that innocent endearments are not to be exceeded."

Spencer St. John tells us, in speaking of the piratical and ferocious Sea Dayaks of Borneo, that "besides the ordinary attention which a young man is able to pay to the girl he desires to make his wife—as helping her in her farm work, and in carrying home her load of vegetables or wood, as well as in making her little presents, as a ring or some brass chain-work with which the women adorn their waists, or even a petticoat—there is a very peculiar testimony of regard which is worthy of note. About nine or ten at night, when the family is supposed to be fast asleep within the mosquito curtains in the private apartments, the young man quietly slips back the bolt by which the door is fastened on the inside, and enters the room on tiptoe. On hearing who it is, she rises at once, and they sit conversing together and making arrangements for the future, in the dark, over a plentiful supply of *sirih-leaf*

and *batle-nut,* which it is the gentleman's duty
to provide, for his suit is in a fair way to pros-
per; but if, on the other hand, she rises and
says, 'be good enough to blow up the fire,' or
'light the lamp' (a bamboo filled with resin),
then his hopes are at an end, as that is the usual
form of dismissal. Of course, if this kind of
nocturnal visit is frequently repeated, the parents do not fail to discover it, although it is a
point of honor among them to take no notice
of their visitor; and, if they approve of him,
matters then take their course, but if not, they
use their influence with their daughter to en-
sure the utterance of the fatal 'please blow up
the fire.' "

And now, having discussed the custom of
bundling as it formerly existed in Great
Britain, and having proved its identity with
the *queesting* of Holland, and the *namzat bezé*
of Central Asia, we propose to follow our in-
vestigations to the continent of America, and
to trace, if we can, its origin and progress in the

UNITED STATES OF AMERICA,

in doing which, it is quite likely that, we follow the identical line of travel and coloniza-
tion—viz.: from Old to New England, and
from Netherlands (the father-land) to New
Netherlands—by which the custom of bundling
was really transplanted to these western shores.
For, although the grave and (sometimes) ve-
racious historian of New York, Diedrich
Knickerbocker, hath endeavored to fasten upon
the Connecticut settlers the odium of having
introduced the custom into New Netherland,*

---

* "Great jealousy did they likewise stir up by their inter-
meddling and successes among the divine sex; for being a
race of brisk, likely, pleasant tongued varlets, they soon
seduced the light affections of the simple lasses from their
ponderous Dutch gallants. Among other hideous customs,
they attempted to introduce among them that of *bundling,*
which the Dutch lasses of the Nederlandts, with that eager
passion for novelty and foreign fashions natural to their sex,
seemed very well inclined to follow, but that their mothers,
being more experienced in the world, and better acquainted
with men and things, strenuously discountenanced all such
outlandish innovations."

to the great offense of all properly disposed
people; yet we may reasonably doubt whether
the young mynheers and frauleins of New
Amsterdam, in that day, were any more innocent of this lover's pastime, than their vivacious
Connecticut neighbors. Indeed, can it be for
one moment supposed that the good Hollanders
—a most unchanging and conservative race—
should have been so far false to the traditions
of their fathers, and the honor of the father-
land, as to leave behind them, when they
crossed the seas, the good old custom of *queesting,* with its time-honored associations and delights? Or can it be imagined that those astute
lawgivers and political economists, the early
governors and burgomasters, were so blind to
the necessities and interests of a new and
sparsely populated country, as to forbid bundling within their borders? Indeed, it would
be but a sorry compliment to the wisdom of
that sagacious and far-sighted body of mer-
chants comprised in the High and Mighty West

India Company, to believe that they were unwilling to introduce under their benign auspices, a custom so intimately connected with their own national social habits, and so promising to the prospective interests and enlargements of their *new plantations,* as this. And, truly, Diedrich himself, doth, in another part of his book, inadvertently betray the fact that bundling was by no means a purely Yankee trick, for he speaks of the redoubtable Anthony Van Corlaer — purest of Dutchmen — as "passing through Hartford, and Pyquag, and Middletown, and all the other border towns, twanging his trumpet like a very devil, so that the sweet valleys and banks of the Connecticut resounded with the warlike melody, and stopping occasionally to eat pumpkin pies, dance at country frolics, and *bundle* with the beauteous lasses of those parts, whom he rejoiced exceedingly with his soul-stirring instrument." Which passage, while it proves that the practice of bundling prevailed in Connecticut, proves equally well that Anthony the trumpeter was by no means inexperienced in its delights, nor unwilling to enjoy its comforts, whether under the name of *bundling* or *queesting*.

Indeed, we do most truly believe that the cunning Knickerbocker, in his desire to vindicate, as he thought, the character of his race against the accusation of immorality, hath by his denial not only committed a grievous sin against "the truth of history," but hath greatly added thereto, by attempting to foist off the opprobrium of the same on to the shoulders of the Connecticut folks. But history will not remain forever falsified, and the day has at length arrived when every historical tub must "stand on its own bottom," and the world will henceforth know that the New Netherlanders did not take bundling by inoculation from the Yankees, but that they brought it with them to the New World, as an ancestral heirloom.

This point being thus satisfactorily settled, to the honor of the Dutchman, and the extreme satisfaction of all future historians, we next proceed to investigate the bundling prevalent in

THE NEW ENGLAND STATES,

Where, as we have already shown, it was, as with the Dutchmen, an *inherited* custom. Its comparatively innocent and harmless character has, however, been fearfully distorted and maligned by irresponsible satirists, and prejudiced historians. Take, for example, the following passage from Knickerbocker's *History of New York,** wherein he pretends to describe "the curious device among these sturdy barbarians [the Connecticut colonists], to keep up a harmony of interests, and promote population. * * * They multiplied to a degree which would be incredible to any man unacquainted with the marvellous fecundity of this growing

---

* By Washington Irving, p. 211. 4th Am. edition.

country. This amazing increase may, indeed, be partly ascribed to a singular custom prevalent among them, commonly known by the name of *bundling*—a superstitious rite observed by the young people of both sexes, with which they usually terminated their festivities, and which was kept up with religious strictness by the more bigoted and vulgar part of the community. This ceremony was likewise, in those primitive times, considered as an indispensable preliminary to matrimony; their courtships commencing where ours usually finish, by which means they acquired, that intimate acquaintance with each other's good qualities before marriage, which has been pronounced · by philosophers the sure basis of a happy union. Thus early did this cunning and ingenious people display a shrewdness at making a bargain, which has ever since distinguished them, and a strict adherence to the good old vulgar maxim about 'buying a pig in a poke.'

"To this sagacious custom, therefore, do I chiefly attribute the unparalleled increase of the Yanokie or Yankee tribe; for it is a certain fact, well authenticated by court records and parish registers, that wherever the practice of bundling prevailed, there was an amazing number of sturdy brats annually born unto the state, without the license of the law, or the benefit of clergy. Neither did the irregularity of their birth operate in the least to their disparagement. On the contrary, they grew up a long-sided, raw-boned, hardy race of whoreson whalers, wood-cutters, fishermen, and peddlers; and strapping corn-fed wenches, who by their united efforts tended marvellously towards populating those notable tracts of country called Nantucket, Piscataway, and Cape Cod."

Hear, also, that learned, but audacious and unscrupulous divine, the Rev. Samuel Peters, who thus discourseth at length upon the custom of bundling in Connecticut, and other parts of New England. After admitting that "the women of Connecticut are strictly virtuous, and to be compared to the prude rather than the European polite lady," he says:

"Notwithstanding the modesty of the females is such that it would be accounted the greatest rudeness for a gentleman to speak before a lady of a garter, knee, or leg, yet it is thought but a piece of civility to ask her to *bundle;* a custom as old as the first settlement in 1634. It is certainly innocent, virtuous and prudent, or the puritans would not have permitted it to prevail among their offspring, for whom in general they would suffer crucifixion. Children brought up with the chastest ideas, with so much religion as to believe that the omniscient God sees them in the dark, and that angels guard them when absent from their parents, will not, nay, cannot, act a wicked thing. People who are influenced more by lust, than a serious faith in God, who is too pure to behold iniquity with approbation, ought never to *bundle.* If any man, thus a stranger to the love of virtue, of God, and the Christian religion, should *bundle* with a young lady in New England, and behave himself unseemly towards her, he must first melt her into passion, and expel heaven, death, and hell, from her mind, or he will undergo the chastisement of negroes turned mad—if he escape with life, it will be owing to the parents flying from their bed to protect him. The Indians, who had this method of courtship when the English arrived among them in 1634, are the most chaste set of people in the world. Concubinage and fornication are vices none of them are addicted to, except such as forsake the laws of Hobbamockow and turn Christians. The savages have taken many female prisoners, carried them back three hundred miles into their country, and kept them several years, and yet not a single instance of their violating the laws of chastity has ever been known. This cannot be said of the French, or of the English, wherever Indian or other women have fallen into their hands.

I am no advocate for temptation; yet must say, that *bundling* has prevailed 160 years in New England, and, I verily believe, with ten times more chastity than the sitting on a sofa. I had daughters, and speak from near forty years' experience. *Bundling* takes place only in cold seasons of the year—the sofa in summer is more dangerous than the bed in winter. About the year 1756, Boston, Salem, Newport, and New York, resolving to be more polite than their ancestors, forbade their daughters *bundling* on the bed with any young men whatever, and introduced a sofa to render courtship more palatable and Turkish, whatever it was owing to, whether to the sofa, or any uncommon excess of the *feu d'esprit,* there went abroad a report that this *raffinage* produced more *natural consequences* than all the *bundling* among the boors with their *rurales pedantes,* through every village in New England besides.

"In 1776, a clergyman from one of the polite towns, went into the country, and preached

against the unchristian custom of young men
and maidens lying together on a bed. He was
no sooner out of the church, than attacked by
a shoal of good old women, with, 'Sir, do you
think we and our daughters are naughty, because we allow *bundling?*' 'You lead yourselves
into temptation by it.' They all replied at once,
'Sir, have you been told thus, or has experience
taught it you?' The Levite began to lift up his
eyes, and to consider of his situation, and bow-
ing, said, 'I have been told so.' The ladies,
una voce, bawled out, 'Your informants, sir,
we conclude, are those city ladies who prefer
a sofa to a bed: we advise you to alter your
sermon, by substituting the word *sofa* for
bundling, and on your return home preach it
to them, for experience has told us that city
folks send more children into the country without fathers or mothers to own them, than are
born among us; therefore, you see, a sofa is
more dangerous than a bed.' The poor priest,
seemingly convinced of his blunder, exclaimed,

'*Nec vitia nostra, nec remedia pati possumus,*
hoping thereby to get rid of his guests; but an
old matron pulled off her spectacles, and, looking the priest in the face like a Roman heroine,
said, '*Noli putare me hæc auribus tuis dare.*'
Others cried out to the priest to explain his
Latin. 'The English,' said he, 'is this: Wo is
me that I sojourn in Meseck, and dwell in the
tents of Kedar!' One pertly retorted, '*Gladii
decussati sunt gemina presbyteri clavis.*' The
priest confessed his error, begged pardon, and
promised never more to preach against bundling, or to think amiss of the custom; the
ladies generously forgave him, and went away.

"It may seem very strange to find this custom
of bundling in bed attended with so much innocence in New England, while in Europe it is
thought not safe or scarcely decent to permit a
young man and maid to be together in private
anywhere. But in this quarter of the old
world the viciousness of the one, and the simplicity of the other, are the result merely of

education and habit. It seems to be a part of heroism, among the polished nations of it, to sacrifice the virtuous fair one, whenever an opportunity offers, and thence it is concluded that the same principles actuate those of the new world. It is egregiously absurd to judge of all countries by one. In Spain, Portugal and Italy, jealousy reigns; in France, England, and Holland, suspicion; in the West and East Indies, lust; in New England, superstition. These four blind deities govern Jews, Turks, Christians, infidels, and heathen. Superstition is the most amiable. She sees no vice with approbation but persecution, and self-preservation is the cause of her seeing that. My insular readers will, I hope, believe me, when I tell them that I have seen, in the West Indies, naked boys and girls, some fifteen or sixteen years of age, waiting at table and at tea, even when twenty or thirty virtuous English ladies were in the room; who were under no more embarrassment at such an awful sight in the eyes of English people that have not traveled abroad, than they would have been at the sight of so many servants in livery. Shall we censure the ladies of the West Indies as vicious above all their sex, on account of this local custom? By no means; for long experience has taught the world that the West Indian white ladies are virtuous prudes. Where superstition reigns, fanaticism will be minister of state; and the people, under the taxation of zeal, will shun what is commonly called vice, with ten times more care than the polite and civilized Christians, who know what is right and what is wrong from reason and revelation. Happy would it be for the world, if reason and revelation were suffered to control the mind and passions of the great and wise men of the earth, as superstition does that of the simple and less polished! When America shall erect societies for the promotion of chastity in Europe, in return for the establishment of European arts in the American capitals, then Europe will discover that there is more Christian philosophy in American bundling than can be found in the customs of nations more polite.

"I should not have said so much about bundling, had not a learned divine* of the English church published his travels through some parts of America, wherein this remarkable custom is represented in an unfavorable light, and as prevailing among the *lower class* of people. The truth is, the custom prevails among all classes, to the great honor of the country, its religion, and ladies. The virtuous may be tempted; but the tempter is despised. Why it should be thought incredible for a young man and young woman innocently and virtuously to lie down together in a bed with a great part of their clothes on, I cannot conceive. Human passions may be alike in every region; but religion, diversified as it is, operates differently

---

* Dr. Andrew Burnaby. *Travels through the Middle Settlements in North America, in the years* 1759 *and '60.* London, 1775.

in different countries. Upon the whole, had I daughters now, I would venture to let them *bundle* on the bed, or even on the sofa, after a proper education, sooner than adopt the Spanish mode of forcing young people to prattle only before the lady's mother the chit-chat of artless lovers. Could the four quarters of the world produce a more chaste, exemplary and beautiful company of wives and daughters than are in Connecticut, I should not have remaining one favorable sentiment for the province. But the soil, the rivers, the ponds, the ten thousand landscapes, together with the virtuous and lovely women which now adorn the ancient kingdoms of Connecticote, Sassacus, and Quinnipiog, would tempt me into the highest wonder and admiration of them, could they once be freed of the skunk, the moping-owl, rattlesnake and fanatic Christian."

Or, to take another example of the abuse heaped by our English cousins upon this so-called "American custom of bundling." We extract the following from an article entitled *British Abuse of American Manners,* published in 1815.* It seems that it had long been a custom in the Westminster school, in the city of London, for the senior students, who were about to leave that seminary for the university, at the age of sixteen to eighteen, to have an annual dramatic performance, which was generally a play of Terence.† To this, as annually performed, there was usually a Latin prologue, and also an epilogue composed for the occasion; and this epilogue turned, for the most part, on the manners of the day that would bear the gentle correction of good humored satire, in elegant Latinity. In the epilogue presented at one of these exhibitions, about 1815, in connection with the performance of

---

* *The Portfolio* (Philadelphia, May 1816), p. 397.

† *Terence's Plays* were preferred to those of Plautus, for this purpose, inasmuch as the latter were more obscure, and abounded in obsoletisms, and therefore Terence was preferred in England as the text-book for schools.

Terence's *Phormio,* the following balderdash
(with much else, as applied to American life
and manners) was introduced and spoken by
these ingenuous and virtuous British youth, before a large and enlightened audience:

"Nec morum dicere promtum est,
Sit ratio simplex, sitne venusta magis.
Æthiopissa palam mensæ formulatur herili
In puris naturalibus, ut loquimur.
Vir braccis se bellus amat nudare décentér,
Strenuus ut choreas ex-que-peditus agat.
Quid quod ibi; quod congere ipsis conque moveri
Dicitur, incolumi nempe pudicitiâ,
Sponte suâ, sine fraude, torum sese audet in unum.
Condere cum casto casta puelle viro?
Quid noctes cœnaque Deûm? quid amœna piorum.
Concilia?"

Which being translated is as follows:

"Nor is it easy to say whether the tenor of their manners
is more to be admired for simplicity or elegance; a negro
wench, as we are told, will wait on her master at table in
native nudity; and a beau will strip himself to the waist,
that he may dance unincumbered, and with more agility.
There, too, we hear of the practice of *bundling* without
any infraction of female modesty; and the chaste maiden,
without any deception, but with right good will, ventures

to share the bed with her chaste swain! Oh, what nights and banquets, worthy of the gods! What delightful customs among these pious people?"

But this spirit of misrepresentation and ridicule, so glaringly apparent in the foregoing extracts, and which has so universally characterized all those British travelers and authors who have attempted to describe our social habits and manners, is fitly rebuked, even as long ago as 1815, by an anonymous writer, whose trenchant pen reminds our British cousins of the old adage concerning "those who live in glass houses," etc.

"From the time of Jack Cade," says he, "to Lord George Gordon, and down to the present day, neither your *grave* or *gay* authorities on the subject of *bundling* and *tarrying* are worthy of criticism. There is a littleness in noticing, in the *London Quarterly Review,* a work which heretofore has been distinguished for its taste, chasteness and celebrity, the observation of travelers who, if men of truth, could only mean to mention customs (if they were customs) of the most vulgar and ignorant, which at any rate are now as little known as are the operation of the blue laws of Connecticut, or part of the penal code enacted to keep in slavery and subjection the sister kingdom.*

"Englishmen, examine your own cottages, particularly in the north, and on the borders, and extend your view to the western extremity of your island. Pray, what term will you give to that promiscuous bundling of the father, mother, children, sons and daughters-in-law, cousins, and inmates who call to *tarry,* and not unfrequently stretch themselves in one common bed of straw on the hovel's floor?†

"Nay, even, in some parts of your empire, the hogs and the cows join the group, and form a most audible respiration from their noses, getting vent through the hole in the roof in-

---

* Ireland.

† *The Reviewers Reviewed, or British Falsehoods detected by American Truths* (New York, published by R. M'Dermot and D. D. Arden, No. 1, City Hotel, Broadway, 1815, 12mo, 72), pp. 34, 35.

tended for a chimney, or spreading throughout the clay built edifice with odorific sweetness, though perhaps not so fragrant and refreshing as was the precious oil poured on the venerable head of Aaron, which Sternhold and Hopkins tell us filled the room with pleasure. In the early settlement of this country there might have been houses in the route of the inquisitive and insidious European travelers, unprovided with a spare bed on which he might stretch his limbs; but, now should Mr. Canning* himself visit us, he need not fear being *bundled*—he need not travel far in any part of the United States without enjoying the luxury of a soft couch and clean sheets, where he can ruminate on the injustice he attempts on our national character."

Badinage, ridicule and misrepresentation aside, however, there can be no reasonable doubt that *bundling* did prevail to a very great

* The Right Honorable Sir George Canning, the editor of the *London Quarterly Review.*

extent in the New England colonies from a very early date. It is equally evident that it was originally confined almost entirely to the lower classes of the community, or to those whose limited means compelled them to economize strictly in their expenditure of firewood and candlelight. Many, perhaps the majority, of the dwellings of the early settlers, consisted of but one room, in which the whole family lived and slept. Yet their innocent and generous hospitality forbade that the stranger, or the friend whom night overtook on their threshold, should be turned shelterless and couchless away, so long as they could offer him even half of a bed. As an example of this we may cite the case of Lieut. Anbury, a British officer, who served in America during the Revolutionary War, and whose letters preserve many sprightly and interesting pictures of the manners and customs of that period. In a letter dated at Cambridge, New England, November 20, 1777, he thus speaks:

"The night before we came to this town [Williamstown, Mass.], being quartered at a small log hut, I was convinced in how innocent a view the Americans look upon that indelicate custom they call *bundling*. Though they have remarkable good feather beds, and are extremely neat and clean, still I preferred my hard mattress, as being accustomed to it; this evening, however, owing to the badness of the roads, and the weakness of my mare, my servant had not arrived with my baggage at the time for retiring to rest. There being only two beds in the house, I inquired which I was to sleep in, when the old woman replied, 'Mr. Ensign,' here I should observe to you, that the New England people are very inquisitive as to the rank you have in the army; 'Mr. Ensign,' says she, 'our Jonathan and I will sleep in this, and our Jemima and you shall sleep in that.' I was much astonished at such a proposal, and offered to sit up all night, when Jonathan immediately replied, 'Oh, la! Mr. Ensign, you

won't be the first man our Jemima has bundled
with, will it Jemima?' when little Jemima,
who, by the bye, was a very pretty, black-eyed
girl, of about sixteen or seventeen, archly replied, 'No, father, not by many, but it will be
with the first Britainer' (the name they give to
Englishmen). In this dilemma what could I
do? The smiling invitation of pretty Jemima
—the eye, the lip, the—Lord ha' mercy, where
am I going to? But wherever I may be going
now, I did not go to bundle with her—in the
same room with her father and mother, my
kind *host* and *hostess* too! I thought of that—
I thought of more besides—to struggle with
the passions of nature; to clasp Jemima in my
arms—to—do what? you'll ask—why, to do—
nothing! for if amid all these temptations, the
lovely Jemima had melted into kindness, she
had been an outcast from the world—treated
with contempt, abused by violence, and left
perhaps to perish! No, Jemima; I could have
endured all this to have been blest with you,

but it was too vast a sacrifice, when you were to be the victim! Suppose how great the test of virtue must be, or how cold the American constitution, when this unaccountable custom is in hospitable repute, and perpetual practice."*

Again, in a subsequent letter, the Lieutenant, after describing a New England sleighing frolic, says: "In England this would be esteemed extremely imprudent, and attended with dangerous consequences; but, after what I have related respecting *bundling,* I need not say, in how innocent a view this is looked upon. Apropos, as to that custom, along the sea coast, by a continual intercourse among Europeans, it is in some measure abolished; but they still retain one something similar, which is termed *tarrying.* When a young man is enamored of a woman, and wishes to marry her, he proposes the affair to her parents (without whose consent

---

* *Travels through the Interior Parts of America; in a Series of Letters* (by an officer; a new edition, London, 1781, 8vo), vol. II, pp. 37-40.

no marriage, in this colony, can take place); if
they have no objections, he is allowed to tarry
with her one night, in order to make his court.
At the usual time the old couple retire to bed,
leaving the young ones to settle matters as they
can, who having sat up as long as they think
proper, get into bed together also, but without
putting off their under garments, to prevent
scandal. If the parties agree, it is all very well,
the banns are published, and they married without delay; if not, they part, and possibly never
see each other again, unless, which is an accident that seldom happens, the forsaken fair
proves pregnant, in which case the man, unless
he absconds, is obliged to marry her, on pain of
excommunication."*

The word *tarry,* in the sense of *to stop* or *to
stay,* was more used by our ancestors than by
the present generation; yet we think that Lieut.
Aubury was mistaken in his idea that the *tarry-*

---

* *Anbury's Travels,* pp. 87, 88.

ing was but for a single night. It is true that marriages were early, and probably the courtships were short, but we all know enough of New England *sparking* to know that a single night was cutting it rather short; and yet it is easy to see how Anbury should get his erroneous idea. True, if the lover was so unlucky as to get his final dismissal the first night, there was an end of the matter, and well might they fail to meet again; but, in that case, it is not likely that the favors of which he could boast would be such as to seriously affect the reputation of the girl with whom he tarried. The fact that in the custom of *tarrying,* the parties also *bundled,* does not authorize the synonymous use of the two words, which have nothing in common. For, doubtless many young men *tarried* with their sweethearts, who did not *bundle* with them.

Again, when, on a sabbath night, the faithful swain arrived, having, perhaps walked ten or more weary miles, to enjoy the company of his

favorite lass, in the few brief hours which
would elapse before the morning light should
call him again to his homeward walk and his
week of toil, was it not the dictate of humanity
as well as of economy, which prompted the *old
folks* to allow the approved and accepted suitor
of their daughter to pursue his wooing under
the downy coverlid of a good feather bed
(oftentimes, too, in the very same room in
which they themselves slept), rather than to
have them *sit up* and *burn out uselessly* firewood and candles, to say nothing of the risk
of catching their *death o' cold?* Indeed, was
not the sanction of bundling in such cases a
tacit admission, on the part of the parents, of
their perfect confidence in the young folks,
which necessarily acted upon the latter as, at
once, a strong restraint from wrong, and a
strong incentive to right doing? The influence
of early religious training, the powerful control which the church had obtained upon the
social and domestic life of the people, and the

superstitious aspect which, in those days, the gospel was made to wear, must also be taken into the account. And, moreover, is it not probable that the universality of the custom, which certainly cleared it from anything like odium or reproach, would naturally tend to preclude, in a degree, any improper ideas in the minds of those who practiced it? Such, then, we consider the *status* of the custom in the earlier history of the colonies, and among the *first generation* of settlers.

"But," if the reader will allow us to quote from a previous work, "the emigration from a civilized to a new country,* is necessarily a step backward into barbarism. The *second generation* did not fill the places of the fathers. Reared amid the trials and dangers of a new settlement, they were in a great measure deprived of the advantages, both social and educational, which their parents had enjoyed.

---

* *History and Genealogies of Ancient Windsor, Conn.,* p. 495.

Nearly all of the former could write, which cannot be said of their children. Neither did the latter possess that depth of religious feeling, or earnest practical piety which distinguished the first comers. Religion was to them less a matter of the heart than of social privilege, and in the *half way covenant* controversy we behold the gradual *letting down of bars* between a pure church and a grasping world.

"The *third* generation followed in the footsteps of their predecessors. Then came war; and young New England brought from the long Canadian campaigns, stores of loose camp vices, and recklessness, which soon flooded the land with immorality and infidelity. The church was neglected, drunkenness fearfully increased, and social life was sadly corrupted."*

---

* The Rev. Alonzo B. Chapin, in his *History of Ancient Glastenbury, Conn.* (p. 80), says that the church records, during the pastorate of the Rev. John Eels [1759-1791], "compel us to believe that the influence of the French war had been as unfavorable to morals as destructive to life; and that the absurd practice of *bundling* prevalent in those days,

It is not, therefore, a matter of surprise that
bundling should, in the increased laxity of pub-

---

was not infrequently attended with the consequences that
might have been expected, and that both together, aided by
a previous growing laxity of morals, and accelerated by many
concurrent cases, had rolled a tide of immorality over the
land, which not even the bulwark of the church had been
able to withstand. The church records of the first society,
from 1760 to 1790, raise presumptions of the strongest kind,
that then, as since, *incontinence* and *intemperance* were
among the sins of the people. What the condition of things
in Eastbury [an ecclesiastical society in the east part of
Glastenbury] was, we have no means of knowing, *as that
portion of the church records which treats of this point, was
long ago* carefully *removed.* [N.B. Italics are our own.]
There is no reason, however, to suppose that this state of
things was peculiar to Glastenbury, for there is too much
evidence that it prevailed throughout the country."

Mr. Chapin's deductions from the revelations of the
Glastenbury records, will be fully justified by the experience
and observation of every antiquarian who has had occasion to
dig deep among the civil and ecclesiastical records of almost
any one of the older towns of New England. We have before us, while writing, a copy, made some years since, by
ourselves, of the records of the first church of Woodstock,
Conn., covering the period from 1727 to 1777, in which are
a large number of entries, mostly the names of parties who
made *confessions* of this sort before that church. These cases
occur most frequently between the years 1737 and 1770.

lic morals, become more frequently abused. Its pernicious effects became constantly more apparent, and more decidedly challenged the attention of the comparatively few godly men who endeavored to stem and to control the rapidly widening current of immorality which threatened to overwhelm the land.* The power-

---

Our own observations among the records of the old churches in Windsor and East Windsor, is, in effect, the same, and we have occasionally happened upon the original manuscript confessions of individuals read to the church before they were formally admitted to its communion.

* *History of Dedham, Mass.* (by Erastus Worthington, 1827), page 108. Under ministry of Rev. Jason Haven, ordained February 6, 1756.

"Revolutionary times having produced a disposition to investigate all the former principles and opinions of men, in politics and church government, Mr. Haven caused the mode of admission into the church to be altered. This was done in 1793. The new method required the candidate to be propounded to the congregation by the minister. If no objections within fourteen days were made, he was then of course admitted. At the same time the church covenant and creed was altered, and made very general in its expressions. This creed had so few articles, that all persons professing and calling themselves Christians, would assent to it without any objections. The church had ever in this place required

ful intellect of Jonathan Edwards thundered its anathemas upon it; pious divines prayed

---

of its members guilty of unlawful cohabitation before marriage, a public confession of that crime before the whole congregation. The offending female stood in the broad aisle beside the partner of her guilt. If they had been married, the declaration of the man was silently assented to by the woman. This had always been a delicate and difficult subject for church discipline. The public confession, if it operated as a corrective, likewise produced merriment with the profane. I have seen no instance of a public confession for this fault, until the ministry of Mr. Dexter [1724-1755], and then they were extremely rare. In 1781 the church gave the confessing parties the privilege of making a private confession to the church, in the room of a public confession. In Mr. Haven's ministry, the number of cases of unlawful cohabitation increased to an alarming degree. For twenty-five years before 1781, twenty-five cases had been publicly acknowledged before the congregation, and fourteen cases within the last ten years. This brought out the minister to preach on the subject from the pulpit. Mr. Haven, in a long and memorable discourse, sought out the cause of the growing sin, and suggested the proper remedy. He attributed the frequent recurrence of the fault to the custom then prevalent, of females admitting young men to their beds, who sought their company with intentions of marriage. And he exhorted all to abandon that custom, and no longer expose themselves to temptations which so many were found unable to resist.

against it in their closets, and wrestled with it
in their pulpits; while many attempted by a re-
vision of their church polity, by greater care-
fulness in the admission of members; by rules
more stringently framed and enforced, to preserve, as best they might, the purity of the
churches committed to their charge, and to
make them, if it were possible, beacon lights

"The immediate effect of this discourse on the congregation has been described to me, and was such as we must
naturally suppose it would be. A grave man, the beloved
and revered pastor of the congregation, comes out suddenly
on his audience, and discusses a subject on which mirth and
merriment only had been heard, and denounces a favorite
custom. The females blushed and hung down their heads.
The men, too, hung down their heads, and now and then
looked out from under their fallen eyebrows, to observe how
others supported the attack. If the outward appearance of
the assembly was somewhat composed, there was a violent
internal agitation in many minds. And now, when forty-five
years have expired, the persons who were present at the
delivery of that sermon, express its effects by saying: 'How
queerly I felt!' 'What a time it was!' 'This was close
preaching indeed!' The custom was abandoned. The sexes
learned to cultivate the proper degree of delicacy in their intercourse, and instances of unlawful cohabitation in this
town since that time have been extremely rare."

amid the surrounding darkness of the times.* The task, however, was well nigh hopeless. The French wars were succeeded by that of the American Revolution, and not before the close of that struggle, may the custom of bun-

---

* *Butler's History of Groton* (Pepperell & Shirley), page 174. At a church meeting, Feb. 29, 1739-40, the subject of compelling persons to confess themselves guilty of an offense, of which they said, "if not absolutely, yet next to impossible to convict them," was acted upon, and some relaxation made in the rule before adopted; but a part of the record is so worn as to be illegible.

Page 177. June 1, 1761. "The church also at this meeting, voted in relation to the confession necessary to be made by parents, to entitle their children to the rite of baptism, who might be supposed to have committed the offence of which, in Mr. Trowbridge's time, they supposed that, 'if not absolutely, yet next to impossible to convict them,' not materially varying from a *seven-months* rule heretofore adopted. These regulations were signed by the moderator, and assented to by the pastor elect."

Page 181. "During Mr. Dana's ministry [1761-1775] 124 persons (38 males, 86 females) were admitted to the church in full communion; 200 (77 males, 123 females) owned the baptismal covenant. Of the first class, 14 confessed having committed the offence aforementioned, and of the last class, 66, a proportion not indicative of good customs and morals."

dling be said to have received its death-blow, and even then it *died hard*.

Its final disuse was brought about by a variety of causes, among which may be named the improved condition of the people after the Revolution, enabling many to live in larger and better warmed houses, and in the very few places where the ministers dared to touch the subject in the pulpit, as in Dedham, already referred to, a decided effect was produced, but it was confined to the neighborhood, having very little effect on the general custom. Probably no single thing tended so much to break up the practice as the publication of a song, or ballad, in an almanac, about 1785.

This ballad described in a free and easy style the various plans adopted by those who bundled, and rather more than hinted at the results in certain cases. Being published in an almanac, it had a much larger circulation than could have been obtained for it in any other way (tract societies not being then in vogue), and the descriptions were so *pat,* that each one who saw them was disposed to apply them in a joking way to any other who was known to practice bundling; and the result was, such a general storm of banter and ridicule that no girl had the courage to stand against it, and continue to admit her lovers to her bed.

We have found many persons who distinctly remember the publication of this song, and the effect which it had on the public mind, but all our efforts to find the almanac containing it, have proved of no avail.

We have, however, been favored with the use of a broadside copy of a ballad, preserved among the treasures of the American Antiquarian Society, at Worchester, Massachusetts, which several of our ancient friends have recognized as identical with that in the almanac, one of them proving it by repeating from memory several lines from the Almanac version, which were precisely like that of the broadside, a copy of which we give herewith.

A NEW BUNDLING SONG;

Or a reproof to those Young Country Women, who follow that reproachful Practice, and to their Mothers for upholding them therein.

Since bundling very much abounds,
In many parts in country towns,
No doubt but some will spurn my song,
And say I'd better hold my tongue;
But none I'm sure will take offence,
Or deem my song impertinence,
But only those who guilty be,
And plainly here their pictures see.
Some maidens say, if through the nation,
Bundling should quite go out of fashion,
Courtship would lose its sweets; and they
Could have no fun till wedding day.
It shant be so, they rage and storm,
And country girls in clusters swarm,
And fly and buz, like angry bees,
And vow they'll bundle when they please.
Some mothers too, will plead their cause,

And give their daughters great applause,
And tell them, 'tis no sin nor shame,
For we, your mothers, did the same;
We hope the custom ne'er will alter,
But wish its enemies a halter.
Dissatisfaction great appear'd,
In several places where they've heard
Their preacher's bold, aloud disclaim
That bundling is a burning shame;
This too was cause of direful rout
And talk'd and told of, all about,
That ministers should disapprove
Sparks courting in a bed of love,
So justified the custom more,
Than e'er was heard or known before.
The pulpit then it seems must yield,
And female valor take the field,
In places where their custom long
Increasing strength has grown so strong;
When mothers herein bear a sway,
And daughters joyfully obey.
And young men highly pleased too,

Good Lord! what can't the devil do.
Can this vile practice ne'er be broke?
Is there no way to give a stroke,
To wound it or to strike it dead,
And girls with sparks not go to bed.
'Twill strike them more than preacher's tongue,
To let the world know what they've done,
And let it be in common fame,
Held up to view a noted shame.
Young miss if this your practice be,
I'll teach you now yourself to see:
You plead you're honest, modest too,
But such a plea will never do;
For how can modesty consist,
With shameful practice such as this?
I'll give your answer to the life:
"You don't undress, like man and wife."
That is your plea, I'll freely own,
But whose your bondsmen when alone,
That further rules you will not break,
And marriage liberties partake?
Some really do, as I suppose,

Upon design keep on some clothes,
And yet in truth I'm not afraid
For to describe a bundling maid;
She'll sometimes say when she lies down,
She can't be cumber'd with a gown,
And that the weather is so warm,
To take it off can be no harm:
The girl it seems had been at strift;
For widest bosom to her shift,
She gownless, when the bed they're in,
The spark, nought feels but naked skin.
But she is modest, also chaste,
While only bare from neck to waist,
And he of boasted freedom sings,
Of all above her apron strings.
And where such freedoms great are shar'd
And further freedoms feebly bar'd,
I leave for others to relate,
How long she'll keep her virgin state.
Another pretty lass we'll scan,
That loves to bundle with a man,
For many different ways they take,

Through modest rules they all will break.
Some clothes I'll keep on, she will say,
For that has aways been my way,
Nor would I be quite naked found,
With spark in bed, for thousand pound.
But petticoats, I've always said,
Were never made to wear in bed,
I'll take them off, keep on my gown,
And then I dare defy the town,
To charge me with immodesty,
While I so ever cautious be.
The spark was pleased with his maid,
Of apprehension quick he said,
Her witty scheme was keen he swore,
Lying in gown open before.
Another maid when in the dark,
Going to bed with her dear spark,
She'll tell him that 'tis rather shocking,
To bundle in with shoes and stockings.
Nor scrupling but she's quite discreet,
Lying with naked legs and feet,
With petticoat so thin and short,

That she is scarce the better for't;
But you will say that I'm unfair,
That some who bundle take more care,
For some we may with truth suppose,
Bundle in bed with all their clothes.
But bundler's clothes are no defence,
Unruly horses push the fence;
A certain fact I'll now relate,
That's true indeed without debate.
A bundling couple went to bed,
With all their clothes from foot to head,
That the defence might seem complete,
Each one was wrapped in a sheet.
But O! this bundlin's such a witch
The man of her did catch the itch,
And so provoked was the wretch,
That she of him a bastard catch'd.
Ye bundle misses don't you blush,
You hang your heads and bid me hush.
If you wont tell me how you feel,
I'll ask your sparks, they best can tell.
But it is custom you will say,

And custom always bears the sway,
If I wont take my sparks to bed,
A laughing stock I shall be made;
A vulgar custom 'tis, I own,
Admir'd by many a slut and clown,
But 'tis a method of proceeding,
As much abhorr'd by those of breeding.
You're welcome to the lines I've penn'd,
For they were written by a friend,
Who'll think himself quite well rewarded,
If this vile practice is discarded.

The party in favor of bundling were able, too, to *keep a poet,* as is shown by the following ballad, which we transcribe from a printed copy preserved by the American Antiquarian Society.

A NEW SONG
IN FAVOUR OF COURTING

Adam at first was form'd of dust,
  As scripture doth record;
And did receive a wife call'd Eve,
  From his Creator Lord.

From Adam's side a crooked bride,
  The Lord was pleas'd to form;
Ordain'd that they in bed might lay
  To keep each other warm.

To court indeed they had no need,
  She was his wife at first,
And she was made to be his aid,
  Whose origin was dust.

This new made pair full happy were,
  And happy might remain'd,

If his helpmate had never ate,
   The fruit that was restrain'd.

Tho' Adam's wife destroy'd his life,
   In manner that was awful;
Yet marriage now we all allow
   To be both just and lawful.

But women must be courted first,
   Because it is the fashion,
And so at times commit great crimes.
   Caus'd by a lustful passion.

And now a days there are two ways,
   Which of the two is right,
To lie between sheets sweet and clean,
   Or sit up all the night?

But some suppose bundling in clothes
   Do heaven sorely vex;
Then let me know which way to go,
   To court the female sex.

Whether they must be hugg'd or kiss'd
   When sitting by the fire
Or whether they in bed may lay,
   Which doth the Lord require?

But some pretend to recommend
   The sitting up all night;
Courting in chairs as doth appear
   To them to be most right.

Nature's request is, grant me rest,
   Our bodies seek repose;
Night is the time, and 'tis no crime
   To bundle in your clothes.

Since in a bed a man and maid,
   May bundle and be chaste,
It does no good to burn out wood,
   It is a needless waste.

Let coats and gowns be laid aside,
   And breeches take their flight,

An honest man and woman can
  Lay quiet all the night.

In Genesis no knowledge is
  Of this thing to be got,
Whether young men did bundle then,
  Or whether they did not.

The sacred book says wives they took,
  It don't say how they courted,
Whether that they in bed did lay,
  Or by the fire sported.

But some do hold in times of old,
  That those about to wed,
Spent not the night, nor yet the light
  By fire, or in the bed.

They only meant to say they sent
  A man to choose a bride,
Isaac did so, but let me know
  Of any one beside.

Man don't pretend to trust a friend,
  To choose him sheep and cows,
Much less a wife which all his life
  He doth expect to house.

Since it doth stand each man in hand,
  To happify his life,
I would advise each to be wise,
  And choose a prudent wife.

Since bundling is not the thing,
  That judgments will procure,
Go on young men and bundle then,
  But keep your bodies pure.

(Printed and sold by Nathaniel Coverly, Jun. Boston.)

The foregoing version is evidently not complete, several verses having been left out on account of their containing *more truth than poetry*, but these may be supplied from a manuscript copy, evidently made from memory, with considerable variations from the printed copy, which by no means improve it, though the schoolmaster did his best, and probably saved for us a very complete version of the ballad as it passed from mouth to mouth before the printed copy was made.

It was transcribed from a volume of manuscript ballads in the handwriting of Israel Perkins, of Connecticut, written in 1786, when he was eighteen years old, and teaching school.

THE WHORE ON THE SNOW CRUST.

1. Adam at first was formed of dust,
     As we find on record;
   And did receive a wife call'd Eve,
     By a creative word.

2. From Adam's side a crooked bride,
     We find complete in form;
   Ordained that they in bed might lay
     And keep each other warm.

3. To court indeed they had no need,
   She was his wife at first,
And she was made to be his aid,
   Whose origin was dust.

4. This new made pair full happy were,
   And happy might remained,
If his helpmeet had never eat
   The fruit that was restrained.

5. Tho' Adam's wife destroyed his life
   In manner that is awful;
Yet marriage now we all allow
   To be both just and lawful.

6. And now a days there is two ways,
   Which of the two is right:
To lie between sheets sweet and clean
   Or sit up all the night.

7. But some suppose bundling in clothes
   The good and wise doth vex;

Then let me know which way to go
To court the fairer sex.

8. Whether they must be hugg'd and buss'd
When sitting up all night;
Or whether they in bed may lay,
Which doth reason invite?.

9. Nature's request is, give me rest,
Our bodies seek repose;
Night is the time, and 'tis no crime
To bundle in our clothes.

10. Since in a bed a man and maid
May bundle and be chaste;
It doth no good to burn up wood
It is a needless waste.

11. Let coat and shift be turned adrift,
And breeches take their flight,
An honest man and virgin can
Lie quiet all the night.

12. But if there be dishonesty
      Implanted in the mind,
   Breeches nor smocks, nor scarce padlocks
      The rage of lust can bind.

13. Kate, Nance and Sue proved just and true,
      Tho' bundling did practise;
   But Ruth beguil'd and proved with child,
      Who bundling did despise.

14. Whores will be whores, and on the floor
      Where many has been laid,
   To sit and smoke and ashes poke,
      Won't keep awake a maid.

15. Bastards are not at all times got
      In feather beds we know;
   The strumpet's oath convinces both
      Oft times it is not so.

16. One whorish dame, I fear to name
      Lest I should give offence,

But in this town she was took down
   Not more than eight months since.

17. She was the first, that on snow crust,
   I ever knew to gender;
I'll hint no more about this whore
   For fear I should offend her.

18. 'Twas on the snow when Sol was low,
   And was in Capricorn,
A child was got, and it will not
   Be long ere it is born.

19. Now unto those that do oppose
   The bundling trade, I say
Perhaps there's more got on the floor,
   Than any other way.

20. In ancient books no knowledge is
   Of these things to be got;
Whether young men did bundle then,
   Or whether they did not.

21. Since ancient book says wife they took,
      It don't say how they courted;
   Whether young men did bundle then,
      Or by the fire sported.

   [But some do hold in times of old,
      That those about to wed,
   Spent not the night, nor yet the light,
      By fire, or in the bed.]

22. They only meant to say they sent
      A man to choose a bride;
   Isaac was so, but let me know,
      If any one beside.

23. Men don't pretend to trust a friend
      To choose him sheep or cows;
   Much more a wife whom all his life
      He does expect to house.

24. Since it doth stand each one in hand
      To happyfy his life;

I would advise each to be wise,
And choose a prudent wife.

25. Since bundling is not a thing
That judgment will procure;
Go on young men and bundle then,
But keep your bodies pure.

Since this work went to press we have been favored, by one of our antiquarian friends in Massachusetts, with a copy of another poetical blast against the practice of bundling. It was written in the latter part of the last, or the first decade of the present century*, by a learned and distinguished clergyman settled in Bristol county, Massachusetts, who was a graduate of Harvard University, and a doctor of divinity. The original manuscript from which our copy

---

* The first edition of Stiles' History of Bundling appeared in 1871.

is made, is very carefully written out, with corrections apparently of a later date, and now undoubtedly appears for the first time in printed form.

A POEM AGAINST BUNDLING.

Dedicated to ye Youth of both Sexes

1. Hail giddy youth, inclined to mirth,
    To guilty amours prone,
 Come blush with me, to think and see
    How shameless you are grown.

2. 'Tis not amiss to court and kiss,
    Nor friendship do we blame,
 But bundling in, women with men,
    Upon the bed of shame;

3. And there to lay till break of day,
    And think it is no sin,
 Because a smock and petticoat
    Have chanced to lie between.

4. Such rank disgrace and scandal base,
   All modest youth will shun,
For 'twill infest, like plague or pest,
   And you will be undone.

5. Let boars and swine lie down and twine,
   And grunt, and sleep, and snore,
But modest girls should not wear tails
   Nor bristles any more.

6. Let rams the sheep mount up and leap,
   Without restraint or blame,
But will young men act just like them?
   Oh, 'tis a burning shame!

7. It is not strange that horses range
   Unfettered to the last,
But youthful lusts in fetters must
   Be chained to virtue fast.

8. Dogs and bitches wear no breeches,
   Clothing for man was made,

Yet men and women strip to their linen,
 And tumble into bed.

9. Yes, brutal youth, it is the truth,
 Your modesty is gone,
And could you blush, you'd think as much,
 And curse what you have done.

10. To have done so some years ago,
 Was counted more disgrace
Than 'tis of late to propagate
 A spurious bastard race.

11. Quit human kind and herd with swine,
 Confess yourself an whore;
Go fill the stye, there live and die,
 Or never bundle more.

12. Shall gentlemen with ladies join
 To practice like the brutes,
Then let them keep with cattle and sheep,
 And fodder on their fruits.

13. This cursed course is one great source
    Of matches undesigned,
    Quarrels and strife twixt man and wife,
    And bastards of their kind.

14. But in excuse of this abuse
    It oftentimes is said,
    Father and mother did no other
    Than strip and go to bed.

15. But grant some did as you have said,
    Yet do they not repent,
    And wish that you may never do
    What they so much lament?

16. A stupid ass can't be more base,
    Than are those guilty youth
    Who fill with smart a parent's heart,
    And turn it into mirth.

17. Others do plead hard for the bed,
    Their health and weariness,

So drunkards will drink down their swill,
And call it no excess.

18. Under pretense of self defense,
Others will scold and say,
An honest maid is chaste abed
As any other way.

19. But where's the man that fire can
Into his bosom take,
Or go through coals on his foot soles
And not a blister make?

20. Temptation's way has led astray
The likeliest of you all,
And yet you're found on slippery ground,
And think you cannot fall.

21. A female meek, with blushing cheek,
Seized in some lover's arms,
Has oft grown weak with Cupid's heat,
And lost her virgin charms.

22. But last of all, up speaks romp Moll
    And pleads to be excused,
For how can she e'er married be,
    If bundling be refused?

23. What strange mistake young women make,
    To hope for sparks this way!
Your fond bold acts can't lay a tax
    That men will ever pay.

24. So cheap and free some women be,
    That men are cloyed with sweet,
As horse or cow starve at the mow
    With fodder under feet.

25. 'Tis therefore vain yourselves to screen,
    The practice is accurst,
It is condemned by God and man,
    The pious and the just.

26. Should you go on, the day will come,
    When Christ your Judge will say,

In *bundles* bind each of this kind,
　　And cast them all away.

27. Down deep in hell there let them dwell,
　　And bundle on that bed;
There burn and roll without control,
　　'Till all their lusts are fed.

The evidence presented in the preceding pages, establishes, as we think, the following facts:

1st. That the custom, so far as it pertained to the American States, had its origin as a matter of convenience and necessity.

2d. That in all stages of its history it was chiefly confined to the humbler classes of society.

3d. That its prevalence may be said to have closed with the eighteenth century.

It is our opinion that it came nearest to being a universal custom from 1750 to 1780, and that it was, at all times, regarded by the better

classes as a serious evil, and was no more countenanced by them than the frequenting of grog
shops is by the better class of the present day.

This opinion is corroborated by the remarks
of several old persons whom we have consulted
as to their recollections of the custom. Among
these, Mr. B., of East Haddam, Ct., now in his
95th year, says that he well remembers it; that
it could not be called general, though frequent.
It was not practiced among the more intelli-
gent, educated classes, nor among those who
lived in large, well warmed houses. He says it
was not the fashion to bundle with any chap
who might call on a girl, but that it was a spe-
cial favor, granted only to a favorite lover, who
might consider it a proof of the high regard
which the damsel had for him; in short, it was
only accepted lovers who were thus admitted to
the bed of the fair one, and, as he expresses it,
only after long continued urging in most cases.*

---

* But this was as late as 1785 to 1790, when the custom
was very near its end.

He thinks the fashion ceased about 1790 to 1800, and in consequence of education and refinement; and that *no more mischief was done then than there is now-a-days.*

In the same strain, also, spoke the genial Colonel H., a native of Berlin, Ct., born in 1775. He was perfectly conversant with the custom, had known the old ladies, in some cases, to go up stairs before retiring, to see that the bundling couple were comfortable, *tuck 'em up,* and put on more bedclothes! And stoutly assev-erated his belief "that there wasn't any more mischief done in those days than there is now."

Indeed, all the old people with whom we have conversed on the matter, although in some cases a little unwilling to own that they had ever practiced it themselves, were unanimous in their belief that the abuse of chastity under the bundling regime was no more frequent than it is now. One old gentleman of whom we have heard, in reply to the half reproachful, half joking question of his grandson, whether he wasn't ashamed, replied: "Why no! What is the use of sitting up all night and burning out fire and lights, when you could just as well get under kiver and keep warm; and, when you get tired, take a nap and wake up fresh, and go at it again? Why d—n it, there wasn't half as many bastards then as there are now!"*

Even within the present century we have found traces of the continuance of the practice of bundling, though the instances are perhaps few, and in some measure exceptional. Until a very late day the custom (as a matter of convenience) was prevalent among the Dutch settlers of Pennsylvania, and it is not improbable that traces may still continue to exist in some of

---

* Another, when in his 96th year, in speaking of his knowledge of the custom, after answering all inquiries, voluntarily mentioned his own personal experience. "In my younger days," said he, and his voice trembled, more from emotion than age, "I was on the bed with as many as five or six young women, but I thank God, that in all my long life I have never had carnal knowledge of any but my lawfully wedded wives."

the more remote counties of that state. An old schoolmaster who flourished in Glastenbury, Ct., some twenty years ago, when relating his experiences in teaching in southern Pennsylvania, and speaking of *boarding around,* informed us that when for any reason he did not choose to go to his boarding place for the time being, he was accustomed to stop at a tavern kept by an honest old Dutchman. On one occasion, having asked the landlord if he could stay over night, he was told that he could; and after chatting with his host through the evening, was shown to bed. The landlord set down the candle and had gone out of the room, when our friend noticed the only bed in the room was already occupied, and calling to the host, notified him of the fact; when he cried back: "Oh! dat ish only mine taughter; she won't hurt nopoty," and coolly went his way. And our friend affirmed that he found the daughter not only harmless, but also quite competent to take care of herself.

In New England, we believe that Cape Cod has the dubious honor of holding out the longest against the advance of civilization, bundling, as we have it on good authority, having been practiced there as late as 1827.* In Greenwich, New Jersey, it was in vogue in 1816. In the state of New York this custom came under judicial cognizance in the year 1804, when the supreme court held, that although bundling was admitted to be the custom in some parts of the

---

* A physician who kept school *on the Cape* many years ago, says (June, 1869) : "It is forty years since I was engaged on the Cape in teaching school, and a friend of mine then related to me some of his experience in a long career of courtship which included *bundling*. The family left the happy couple alone. After sitting up till nine or ten o'clock, the lady secures the fire, takes a light and retires, saying, you know the way up stairs, turn to the right, etc. At a proper time he follows, finding her nicely snuggled under the bed clothes, having previously put on a very appropriate and secure night dress, made neither like a bloomer or mantilla, but something like a common dress, excepting the lower part, which is furnished with legs, like drawers properly attached. The dress is drawn at the neck and waist with strings tied with a very strong knot, and over this is put the ordinary apparel."

state, it being proven that the parents of the girl, for whose seduction the suit was brought, countenanced her practicing it, they had no right to complain, or ask satisfaction for the consequences, which, the court say, *naturally followed it!"* *

---

* *Caines' Cases,* II, 219; Seger *vs.* Slingerland.

APPENDIX I,

APPENDIX I.

BUNDLING.

[From *The Yankee of* August 13, 1828, published at Portland, Maine, and edited by John Neal.]

BY Rochefoucauld, in accounting for the populousness of Massachusetts, the New Englanders are charged with bundling.

By Chastelleux, whose book I am not able to refer to now, the charge is repeated, and by half a score of other honest, good natured people, who have made books about the New World.

But, if you enquire into the business, you are pretty sure to be told, enquire where you may, that bundling is not known *there,* but somewhere further back in the woods, or further *down east.* Nay, while in every part of the United States the multitude speak of bundling as the habit of their neighbors, either east, west, north, or south, where the witches of the country were *located* about a century ago by the grandfathers of this generation, I, myself, though I have taken trouble enough to learn the truth, have never yet been able to meet with a case of bundling—of bundling proper, I should say—in the United States, nor with but one trustworthy individual who had ever met with so much as one case, and he had met with *but* one, for which he would give his word. These things are trifles; but when they are told in books that are read and trusted to throughout Europe; such books, too, as that of the Marquis de Chastelleux, or that of De Rochefoucauld, it becomes a matter of serious inquiry. The truth must be told, whatever it is, for the truth cannot be so bad, whatever it may be, as the untruth which is now repeated of us.

The travels of Chastelleux are translated by an Englishman who had been a long while in this country. The book was undoubtedly written with great care. by a very honest, able man, who had very good opportunities of knowing the truth; and is now set off by another very honest, able man, who was, if anything, rather partial to America—enough to make one wary of trusting the report of any traveler who does not say in so many words, after establishing a character for himself—I saw this; I heard this; I take nobody's word for what I now say, etc., etc. It would be easy to enumerate a multitude of other stories which are now believed in, about the people of the United States, not only by the people of Europe, and of Great Britain particularly, but by the people of the United States themselves. But a dry catalogue of such things would be of little use.

[Here he refers to the charge reported of New Englanders, that they *eat pork and molasses—pork and molasses* TOGETHER, which is here denied as a ridiculous story. H. R. S.]

They bundle in Wales; bundling there is a serious matter. A lady—a Welsh woman whose word is truth itself—assured me not long ago, that in her country they do not think a bit the worse, of a girl for anticipating her duties, in other words, for being a mother before she has been a wife; they have discovered, perhaps, that cause and effect may be convertible terms; that in such a serious matter, none but a fool would buy a pig in the poke, and that, after all, maternity may lead to marriage there, as marriage leads to maternity here. And why not? for after the establishment of the lying-in hospitals of Russia, the unmarried who bore *children to the state* were proud of the duty, and were looked upon, we are told, with great favor by the public. She added, also, that she was once at a party made up of sixteen or eighteen females, and females of good character, all but one or two of whom were mothers, or had been so, before they were married. By Chastelleux and his English translator it would appear to have been very much the same in America about the years 1780-1-2. It is not so now. To have had a child before marriage would now be fatal to a woman here, whatever might be her condition or beauty; fatal in every shape. No man would have courage to marry her; no woman of character would associate with her. Ask the first individual you meet, above the age of twelve or thirteen here, and you may have the name and history of every poor girl in the neighborhood who has been so unlucky as to have a child of her own without leave, perhaps, within a period of six or eight years in a populous neighborhood of twenty or thirty miles about. A widow with half a score of children, forty years ago, if we may believe Dr. Franklin, was an object for the fortune hunters of America. It is not so now. The demand for widows, and for every sort of ready made family is beginning to be over.

That which is called bundling here, though bad enough, is not a twentieth part so bad. Here it is only a mode of courtship. The parties instead of sitting up together, go to bed together; but go to bed with their clothes on.

This would appear to be a perilous fashion; but I have been assured by the individual above, that he had proof to the contrary; for in the particular case alluded to, the only case I ever heard of on good authority, although he was invited by the parents of a pretty girl who stood near him, to bundle with her, and although he *did* bundle with her, he had every reason to believe, that if he had been very free, or more free than he might have been at a country frolick after they had invited him to escort her, to sit up with her, to dance with her, he would have been treated as a traitor by all parties. He had a fair opportunity of knowing the truth, and he spoke of the matter as if he would prefer the etiquette of sitting up to the etiquette of going to bed with a girl who had been so brought up. He complained of her as a prude. The following communication appears, however, to be one that may be depended on:*

* In reply to a query addressed to Mr. Neal, who is still living at Portland, Maine, as to whether this letter was a

"MR. NEAL—If you wish to know the *truth* about bundling, I think your correspondent V. could tell you all about it—it seems by his confession that he has practiced it on a large scale. I never heard of the thing till about three years ago; an acquaintance of mine had gone to spend the summer with an aunt, who lived somewhere near Sandy river.* The following is a copy of one of her letters while there:

" 'I should have written sooner, so don't think me unkind, for I have been waiting for something to write about. You requested me to give you a faithful description of the country, the manners and customs of the inhabitants, etc. I have not been here quite three months, but I have been everywhere, seen everything, and got

---

bona fide communication, that gentleman says: "It was an actual communication from a correspondent. Who that correspondent was, I never knew, but I never entertained a doubt, and, in fact, find such internal evidence of good faith, that I should ever question the facts set forth."

* Sandy river is near Farmington, Franklin county, Maine.

acquainted with everybody. I shall certainly inform you of everything I have seen or heard that is worth relating.

" 'You remember how you told me, before I left home, that I was so well looking that if I went so far back in the country I should be very much admired and flattered, and have as many lovers as I could wish for. I find it all true. The people here are remarkably kind and attentive to me; they seem to think that I must be something more than common because I have always lived so near Portland.

" 'But I must tell you that since I have been here I have had a beau. You must know that the young men, *in particular,* are very attentive to me. Well, among these is *one* who is considered the finest young man in the place, and well he may be—he owns a good farm, which has a large barn upon it, and a neat two story house, all finished. These are the fruits of his own industry; besides he is remarkably good looking, is very large but well-proportioned, and has a good share of what I call real manly beauty. Soon after my arrival here I was introduced to this man—no, not *introduced* neither, for they never think of such a thing here. They all know me of course, because I am a *stranger*. Some days, three, four, or half a dozen, call to see me, whom I never before saw or heard of; they come and speak to me as if I were an old acquaintance, and I converse with them as freely as if I had always known them from childhood. In this kind of a way I got acquainted with my beau, that *was;* he was very attentive to me from our first meeting. If we happened to be going anywhere in company he was sure to offer me his arm—no, I am wrong again, he never offered me his arm in his life. If you go to walk with a young man here, instead of offering you his arm as the young men do up our way, he either takes your hand in his, or passes one arm around your waist; and this he does with such a provoking, careless honesty, that you cannot for your life be offended with him. Well, I had walked with my Jonathan several times in this kind of style. I confess there was something in him I could not but like—he does not lack for wit, and has a good share of common sense; his language is never studied—he always seems to speak from the heart. So when he asked what sort of a companion he would make, I very candidly answered, that I thought he would make a very agreeable one. "I think just so of you," said he, "and it shall not be my fault," he continued, "if we are not companions for life." "We shall surely make a bargain," said he, after sitting silent a few moments, "so we'll *bundle* tonight." *"Bundle* what?" I asked. *"We* will bundle together," said he; "you surely know what I mean." "I know that our farmers bundle *wheat, cornstalks* and *hay;* do you mean that you want me to help you bundle any of these?" inquired I. "I mean that I want you to stay with me tonight! It is the custom in this place, when a man stays with a girl, if it is warm weather, for them to throw themselves on the bed, outside the bed clothes; if the weather is cold, they crawl under the clothes, then if they have anything to *say,* they say it—when they get tired of talking they go to sleep; this is what we call bundling—now what do you call it in your part of the world?" "We have no such works," answered I; "not amongst respectable people, nor do I think that any people would, that either thought themselves respectable, or wished to be thought so."

" 'Don't be too severe upon us, Miss——, I have always observed that those who *make believe* so much modesty, have in reality but little. I always act as I feel, and speak as I think. I wish you to do the same, but have none of your make-believes with me—you smile—you begin to think you have been a little too scrupulous—you have no objection to bundling *now,* have you?" "Indeed I have." "I am not to be trifled with; so, if you refuse, I have done with you forever." "Then be done as quick as you please, for I'll not bundle with you nor with any other man." "Then farewell, proud girl," said he. "Farewell, honest man," said I, and off he went sure enough.

" 'I have since made inquiries about *bundling,* and find that it is *really* the custom here, and that they think no more harm of it, than we do our way of a young couple sitting up together. I have known an instance since I have been here, of a girl's taking her sweetheart to a neighbor's house and asking for a bed or two to lodge in, or rather to *bundle* in. They had company at her father's, so that their beds were occupied; she thought no harm of it. She and her family are respectable.

" 'Grandmother says bundling was a very common thing in our part of the country, in old times; that most of the first settlers lived in log houses, which seldom had more than one room with a fire place; in this room the old people slept, so if one of their girls had a sweetheart in the winter she must either sit with him in the room where her father and mother slept, or take him into her sleeping room. She would choose the latter for the sake of being alone with him; but sometimes when the cold was very severe, rather than freeze to death, they would crawl under the bed-clothes; and this, after a while, became a habit, a custom, or a fashion. The man that I am going to send this by, is just ready to start, so I cannot stop to write more now. In my next I'll give you a more particular account of the people here. Adieu.'

"*Mr. Editor,* you may be sure that what is related in the foregoing letter is the truth. I know that there is considerable *other* information in it, mixed up with *that* about which you wished to be informed, but I could not very well separate it."

So after all that has been said of the practice of bundling in our country, by foreign writers, travelers, and reviewers—after all the reproach that has been heaped upon us, now that we are able to get at the plain truth, it appears to be, though certainly a bad practice, not half so bad as the junketing and sitting up courtships that are known elsewhere. Nay, more. Though in the present state of society it is a practice that should be utterly discountenanced everywhere, still it would seem to have grown up out of the peculiar circumstances of our first settlers; to be confined *now* to remote and small districts (for I have heard of only three instances, after all my inquiry); and to be rapidly going out of practice. Yet more; there can be no bad intentions, there can be no evil consequences, where respectable and modest women are not ashamed to acknowledge that they bundle. I am anxious to know the truth for the purpose of correcting both the *misrepresentations* that are abroad, and the *practices* that prevail here. Bundling, however, is known in other countries, where they have less excuse, and in Wales where they do *not* bundle, as I have said before, it is no reproach for a woman to have had a child before marriage. It was so in Russia after

Catharine established her lying-in hospitals.

In the next number of *The Yankee* (August 20th) there is the following editorial paragraph:

BUNDLING.

There is a great outcry just now about the paper on bundling which was in the last *Yankee.* Now this very outcry proves the want of the very paper alluded to. The article is about bundling; and people who imagine bundling to be what it is not, a highly improper and unchaste familiarity, are offended with it; but the very purpose of that paper is to show that bundling is not what it is believed to be, that it is neither so common nor so bad, not a fiftieth part so bad as people have imagined.

APPENDIX II.

APPENDIX II.

THAT the customs of courtship in many parts of the United Kingdom at the present day, are precisely what they were on some parts of New England, New Jersey and Pennsylvania, fifty years ago, is evident from the revelations of the *Royal Commission on the Marriage Laws,* in the year 1868. Dr. Strahan, a physician and surgeon, who for nearly forty years has practiced in the Scottish county of Stirling, testifies before the commission, that his attention was first drawn to the subject in consequence of observing the very great extent of immorality among the working classes, not only as evidenced by the large number of illegitimate children, but also by the still larger number of marriages after the woman was with child; and the number of children born within eight months of wedlock. He found, to his astonishment, that among the working classes (*i. e.,* the agricultural laborers), nine out of ten women, when married, either had had illegitimate children, or were pregnant at the time of marriage. "I have," he says, "a large midwifery practice, and I very rarely attend a woman with her first child, where the child is not born within a few months of wedlock, or else she has had an illegitimate child before." He believes it is very common for women to allow themselves to be seduced in the hope of being married. They go on until they are *enceinte,* and then, if the young man is at all a decent fellow, the friends interfere and the marriage is hurried on. The sketch which Dr. Strahan supplies of Scotch courtships, explains all this part of his observation. Young men and women meet together at night, and the ordinary time is the middle of the night, when every one else is in bed. "It is universal," says Dr. Strahan to the commission, "among the working classes, to have this manner of courtship of which I speak; there is no other courtship, in any other form; the fathers and mothers will not allow their daughters to meet a young man in the daytime; the young man never visits the family, but the parents quite allow this; they have done it themselves before, and there is no objection to it. The young man comes, makes a noise at the window; the young woman goes out, they go to some outhouse; or perhaps the young man is admitted to the young woman's bedroom after all are in bed, and there is an hour or two of what is called courtship, but which would more properely be called flirtation, because it is not necessary that there should be any engagement to marry in these cases."

Lord Lyveden inquired: "Do these meetings take place at particular periods, such as harvest time, or is over the whole of the year?"

Answer: "The whole of the year; very commonly the young man visits the young woman once a week."

Lord Chelmsford said: "In England that

would be called *keeping company*. It is a very extraordinary way of keeping company when the parents allow their daughter to go out with the young man at midnight, or the young man to come into her bedroom."

Answer: "Yes; the parents know of no other way of doing it. I have reasoned with the parents often when attending a case of illegitimate birth, pointing out to the parents how it is they have been led on, but they cannot imagine any other way of doing it; their daughters must have husbands, and there is no other way of courting."

Mr. Justice O'Hagan asking—"Does it prevail generally in Scotland?" was answered—"universally among the agricultural laborers."

In reply to an inquiry by Mr. Dunlop, whether these young men lived under any kind of supervision and knowledge of their masters, or whether they could go out and in as they pleased, Dr. Strahan stated that "plowmen, for instance, very often live in *bothies,* or in the farm-house; they get out after all are in bed, out of the window; or, if they live in a bothie, without any trouble. They go to the neighboring farm-house, they knock at the window, the girl comes to the window, and if she know the young man—or, after a little parley, if she does not know him—she either comes out and goes with him to an outhouse, or he comes into her bedroom. You must remember that they have no other means of intercourse."

"That is the point you press so much?"

"Yes; a young woman cannot see either a sweetheart or an acquaintance in any other way. I believe if it was not for fear of being out at night, the girls would visit one another in the same way; they have no other means of visiting; the customs of the country are such that a young man could not be seen going in daylight to visit his sweetheart."

Mr. Justice O'Hagan: "If the father knew that the young man was coming into the house, and knew that he was with his daughter, would he not interfere?"

"He would lie comfortably in his bed, knowing that his daughter was in an outhouse or barn with a young man, for perhaps two hours; shutting his eyes to it in the same way that a person in the higher ranks would shut his eyes to his daughter going out for a walk with a young man."

Dr. Strahan said also: "When you come to the middle class a young man would not marry a girl that had had a child to another man; and very probably he would not marry a girl that had had a child to himself; but in the lower classes it is not so; it is almost universal to marry a woman that has had a child, or that is with child to himself; but it is very frequent to marry a woman that has had a child to another man; the only objection is the burden of the child; the burden of the child might be an obstacle, but the disgrace would be none."

"Is it supposed," asked a commissioner, "that

the woman, by marrying this other man, wipes off her disgrace with the former?"

"Yes; but it is so common that the disgrace is not so much as to prevent the young man marrying her."

The attorney-general: "It is hardly within our inquiry, but still it is interesting to know; can you tell me whether, in these cases, where the woman marries a man who is not the father of her child, any confusion, as to the parent of the previously born child, arises? Are they apt in law, to pass as the children of the subsequent husband?"

"No, I do not think so."

"The distinction is always kept up?"

"The distinction is always kept up; very often the illegitimate child goes by his own father's name, even among the other children; and I do not think there is apt to be any confusion of that kind."

Still, it seems that, in severely Calvinistic Scotia, the church does not wholly wink at this state of things. The sinning couple, after marriage, have to go through a certain whitewashing at church before they are admitted to what are called church privileges. They have to go before a kirk session, consisting of the minister and perhaps half a dozen elders, when they are *admonished*. If the parties are married, they appear but once; if not married, generally three times. They tender themselves for rebuke without invitation, as without it the child cannot be baptized, or admission given to the sacrament. They apply to the minister in private, and confess their fault, and he causes them to be summoned before the church session.

INDEX.

AFRICAN tribes, courtship among, 42.

America, English misrepresentation of, 62.

America, bundling in, 44.

    inherits bundling from Holland, 45.

    bundling not peculiar to, 13.

    bundling universal in 1750, 106.

Ballads against bundling, 81, 100.

    in favor of bundling, 88, 93.

Brychan, a cloth, 23.

Bundling, antiquity of, 14.

Bundling, abuse of, in New England, 75.

    ballads on, 81, 88, 93, 100.

    ceased with eighteenth century, 106.

    confined to the lower classes, 107.

Bundling, described by Lt. Anbury in 1777, 66.

    definition of, 13.

    decision of N. Y. Supreme court on, 111.

    effect of, 75.

    in America, 44.

    in British isles, 14, 22.

    in Cape Cod, 110.

    in Holland, 35.

Bundling in Maine about 1828, 117.

    in New England States, 48.

    in Wales, 23, 115.

    introduced in America from Holland, 45.

    mentioned by Rev. Sam'l Peters, 51.

    mentioned by Washington Irving, 49.

    mentioned by Dr. A. Burnaby, 1759, 58.

    mentioned by Sir Walter Scott, 20.

    not peculiar to America, 13.